FIT LIKE MIN?
WOTCHER?
HOLA!
HEY THERE
BONJOUR!
CHILLOUT!

DICTIONARY
Erm, I think they mean, HELLO!

£4.35

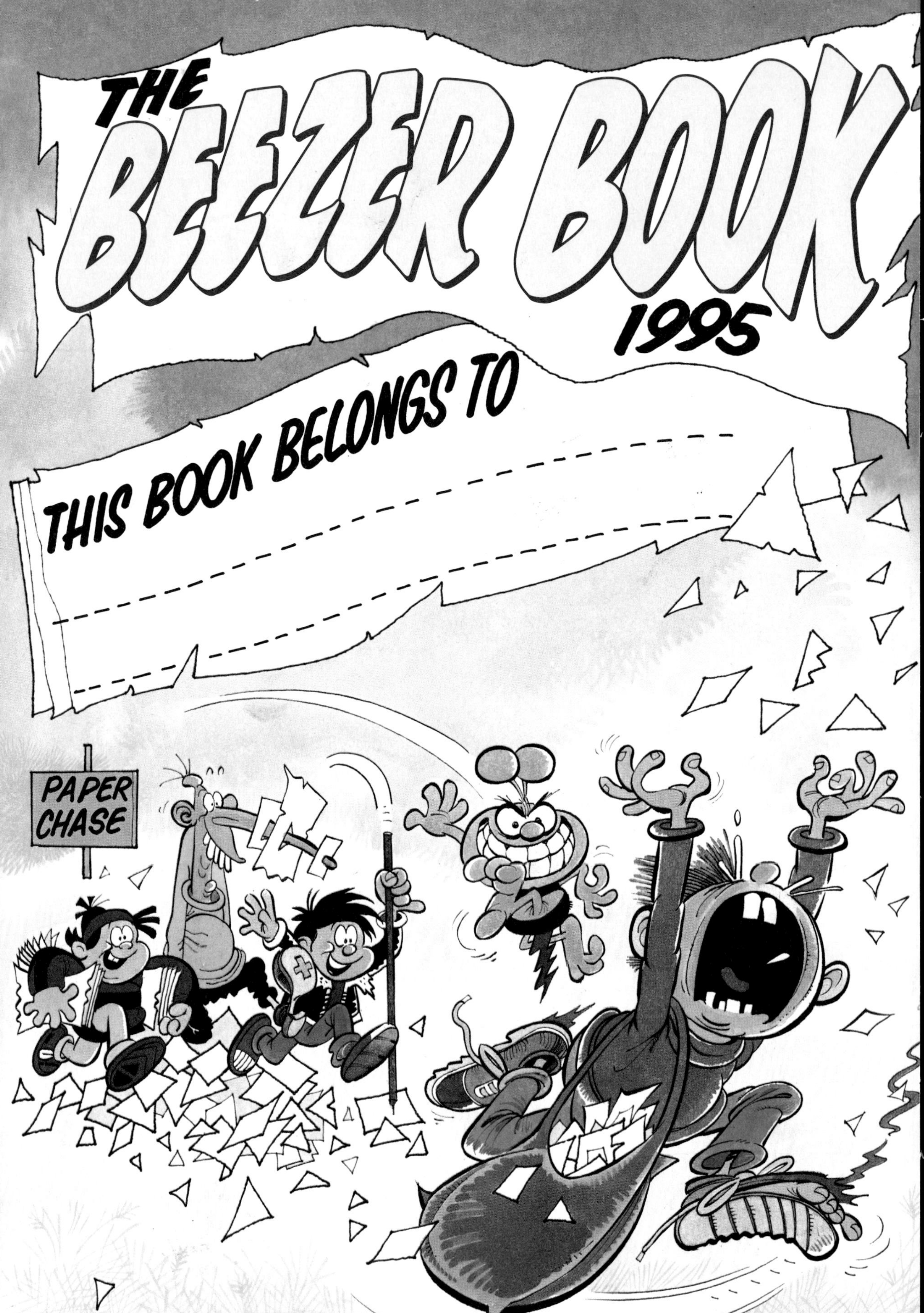

Printed and Published in Great Britain by D. C. THOMSON & CO., LTD., 185 Fleet Street, London, EC4A 2HS.

ISBN 0-85116-580-X

BLINKY

in "OPTICIANS THROUGH THE AGES"

"Early eye-tests could be very hazardous affairs."

OPTICIAN

Bloomin' dark in this cave, isn't it?

"Eye-tests in the Middle Ages took the form of target practice."

"If your aim wasn't good . . ."

"In ancient Egypt, seats for eye-test patients were introduced."

Right lumpy, they are, too!

"In the Dark Ages, nobody could see ANYTHING!"

And that concludes my talk on Opticians Through The Ages. Now — any questions?

Yes . . .

. . . why have you just given your talk in the back of a lorry, behind my new desk?

Er . . . just practising, sir!

DELIVERIES

GEEZER

People only buy CDs and cassettes these days. Nobody wants records — nobody except me, that is.
OLD RECORDS

I'm gonna use 'em to make lots of cash.
GEEZER'S CLAY-PIGEON SHOOTING ONLY £1

It's the best thing that could happen to most of these, if you ask me.
POP!
POP!
POP!
SMASH!
Pull!

Next —
A few splashes of paint and these records look like . . .

. . . a lovely set of plates, selling for only twenty-five quid.
Groovy design.

Should've warned her not to have gravy.
Diddled! There's a hole in the middle.
DRIP!

BEND!
A bend here, and a bend there . . .

Yahoo!
. . . and we've got frisbees — and more money as well.
Gimme!

Bet you can't guess what I'm doing.

There! A cartie with groovy musical wheels.
I'll buy it! Ten quid.

Cackle! The jangle of money is music to my ears.

JINGLE JANGLE

CHINK

Out of my way! I'm trying to break the marathon record.

Eek!

AARGH! MY MONEY!

PLIP!

PLOP!

PLOP!

A VERY long time ago, not far outside the borders of the country that we now call Hungary, lived the ugliest man the world had ever seen. Although his face, with its hairy warts, boils and all manner of scaly bits was dreadful to look at, if you could have seen inside him, his heart was a hundred times uglier. His name was Lazlo, and he loved to wander through the wild woods, breaking birds' eggs, trampling wild flowers and stirring up frog ponds. The odd thing was, that after every wicked deed, Lazlo would become just a fraction more ugly. One of his teeth would turn a slimier shade of green, or his eye would become slightly more bloodshot. It was like a reward for his awfulness.

Now, not far from Lazlo's cottage lived a young seamstress called Katerina, and she vowed she would repay the old man for all his wickedness.

One day when he was out walking she slipped silently into his cottage. She sewed his curtains shut. She sewed up his socks. (Ugh!) She sewed up his bed sheets so he wouldn't be able to climb in. She sewed up his pockets, and his trouser legs.

Before he returned she ran back to her own cottage.

Soon the bellows of rage she heard from the old man told her he was home and had discovered her handiwork. She smiled to herself in her mirror, and something in her reflection drew her attention.

On her cheek was a little hairy wart. "That wasn't there this morning . . ." she said to herself.

Stormin' NORMA

The post has arrived! Anything for me?

Aut
I've always wanted to holiday in our own motor home! Go on, try this one!
Norma! I — hoi!
£10,0

We could drive up to the Scottish highlands and go climbing!
Perish the thought!

Come on, let's see what else we can buy!
Will you list-eek!

FITNESS CENTRE
We could buy this place with your new found wealth!
Howl!

It'd be great! We could work out together every single day!
No! Yerk!

Take me home and we'll have a proper look at that letter!

She allows me no dignity, you know.

It says, 'Dear Sir, you have won two tickets to the new local swimming pool in our prize draw'.
Oh. Won. Pool. Swimming pool.

I just know this is going to be an awful punchline!

WATER let down!
Yup! I was right!

Here's the REAL punchline, Dad! Norma's gone with you for the free swim!
Yeah!
I think I preferred to end on the other awful punchline!
Aargh!
Yaroo!
Dive! Dive! Dive!

ISHARA'S
TESTS OF TIME
To move through the maze, solve each puzzle inside the time limit. At the end, add up all the time you had left and see how you rate.
10
Who lives here?
TIME LIMIT 45 SECONDS
What is the name of Superman's wimpy alter-ego?
TIME LIMIT 60 SECONDS
Name this world famous landmark.
TIME LIMIT 30 SECONDS
Which of these films did Tom Cruise NOT appear in?
FAR AND AWAY
DAYS OF THUNDER
RAIN MAN
GHOST
TOP GUN
TIME LIMIT 60 SECONDS
Geezer's fave subject is money and hidden in the grid are six different national currencies. You have 180 seconds to help Geezer find the loot.
X D O L L A R S
R O O L L L O D
A O D G A X A N
M C Z U N D T U
X N M N C Z E O
Z A A Y W S S P
K R A M O B E O
F F K W I D P T
POUND
DOLLAR
FRANC
MARK
ESCUDO
PESETA
TIME LIMIT 180 SECONDS
Blue Peter has had lots of presenters over the years, including John Leslie, but do you know when the programme started?
1953
1958
1963
1965
1975
1990
TIME LIMIT 60 SECONDS
ANSWERS
The Prime Minister; Clark Kent;
Ghost; Buckingham Palace; 1958.
HOW DID YOU RATE
Under 30 seconds — Dearie dearie me.
31-60 seconds — Not bad — but not good.
Over a minute — Read the Beezer Book again. You deserve it.

STING!
CANTEENA
Z Z Z Z Z Z Z

Hiya, readers — I decided to come to Mexico for my holidays this year — nice an' warm!

Mind you, it's a bit TOO hot for flying!

OOOOOYAH

THIS looks a bit safer as a seat!

But —
Er . . . sorry! I didn't mean to RATTLE you, Mister Snake!
Too bad — you did! SNAP!
Phew! Just missed!
I could do with a drink after all that excitement!
THUD!
WHA — ?
Huh! It's a MIRAGE! That does it!

FREE ICE

Yup! Who needs Mexican chilli when you can have South Pole CHILLY? This is the life!

The
BANANA
BUNCH

Tails — you win.
We'll play against the wind in the first half.
FLIP!

Right! Here we go.

RUMBLE!
SHAKE!
An earthquake!
Nope . . .
SHUDDER

. . . just Fatty's tum rumblin' — we're used to it.
RUMBLE! SQUOYLCH! BLAART!
SHAKE!
QUAKE!

One nil down already, but we'll soon score.
Then —
GRAB!
PHWOOPH!
PHOOM!
An escaped tiger — save us, Lofty!
ZIP!
No, just Fatty's tummy growlin' — ta for the ball.
SWERVE!
Can't help it — I'm hungry.
SQUAARRT! GROOWLL! BLURRRP! GLEURRRK!
TAP!
Goal!

Half-time —
ISH+ CHIPS
HOT DOGS
CURRY
BURGERS
PIZZA
Eat up — we're not gonna be bothered by your tummy in the second half.
BLACK PUDDIN' VINDALOO
MEGA FISH AND CHIPS
Most kind.
GUZZLE SCOFF! CRAM
RED-HOT RADISH AND CHILLI PIZZA
The second half —
I c'n score directly from the kick off now the wind's behind us.
BOOF!
But —
BAARP!
Wah! We're STILL playin' against the pesky wind!
Worra burp! Worra goal!
BLAST!
STOMP! STOMP!

NINO'S father was the most famous guitar maker in all of Spain. When Nino was very young, his father, after the day's work was done, would tell Nino to lay out some bread and cheese for the little helpers who lived under the workshop, and who helped with the guitar making while the rest of the house slept. When Nino grew older, he stopped believing in the little helpers, and would blush when anyone reminded him of the bread and cheese he once left out for them. One hot day, the King of Spain's son ordered a very special guitar from Nino's father. He paid for it with a bag of gold coins, and the guitar was to be ready in a month when it would be the Prince's birthday.

Work started quite well as Nino's father selected the various special pieces of wood which would become the Prince's guitar.

But Nino's father was growing older, and his eyesight was failing, and the work took longer than expected. Nino began to wonder if the instrument would be ready in time.

On the morning before the Prince's birthday, Nino went to waken his father early because there was still much glueing, polishing and tuning to be done. Nino's father had a fever and could not get out of his bed to finish the guitar. All day Nino paced, fretted and worried. The Prince had a terrible temper and might have them thrown in jail.

Night came and the guitar wasn't ready. Nino gave up and prepared to go to bed.

Not that he would sleep much.

A desperate plan came to hir
Hurrying to the kitchen he filled
bowl with bread and cheese, ar
left it in the workshop.

Next morning Nino could hard
believe his eyes. The bread ar
cheese were gone, but the guita
shiny and new had been finishe
and was ready and fit for the Princ

Nino told his father. "Th
helpers came back. They finishe
the guitar."

Nino's father looked at hi
strangely — "But that was just
story for you, Nino. I made it
up . . ."

The Numskulls

GUIDED TOUR

HOWL!
BURRRP!
PAT PAT
RATTLE!
WAAARGH!
These are his Baby-skulls from his childhood. Noisy, they are, too!

WAAH! NO LIKE CABBAGE!
Coo!
SPLAT!

Soon—
That's 'em settled. Sneak out QUIETLY!
ZZZ!
ZZZ!

In here . . .
GUIDE

. . . is the THINK-TANK! It's where all Our Boy's ideas swim about!

YEP! An' I'm goin' for a swim in it!
Nutty! Stop!
GUIDE

Oh-oh!
SPLOOSH!
Goodness knows what all these ideas comin' out at once will do to Our Boy!
WEAR FANCY DRESS
RIDE ON BIKE
HAVE A BATH
KICK A BALL
THIS is what it does!
Next—
Doctors don't know what the appendix is for — but we do!
It's a great punch-bag in our gym!
THUMP!
But it also has ANOTHER use . . .
GUIDE
OI! Quit that! That's sore, y'know! How'd you like me to hit YOU?
. . . 'cos it can be a GRUMBLING appendix . . .
NO SCHOOL TODAY!
. . . an' get us a day off work! Cheerio, readers!
Poor thing!

LITTLE MO

Remember your homework, class.
ESSAY "WHAT I WANT TO BE WHEN I GROW UP"
Hmm. What would I like to be?

A basketball player!

Outta the way, Shorty!

BAKERY
A baker, perhaps.

ROCK CAKES
WHUMP!
Waagh! Too heavy!

GYM
Or a boxer, then!
Easy, know wot ah mean?
C'mere!
SNIPE
Well, Little Mo. What do you want to be when you grow up?
Only one thing.
ESSAY
Haw-haw!
Ha-ha!
BIGGER!
BIGGER

IT'S ONLY A GAME!

It's only a game — but there's more to football than can be seen on the pitch. For a pretty simple game, there's an awful lot of people involved, with all sorts of different ideas about the game. Let's meet just some of them . . .

No, no, no! THIS is how it should be done!

The Fan.

What a game! It's 100 mph end to end stuff! A real ding-dong battle!

The Radio Commentator.

THE GREATEST

The Player.

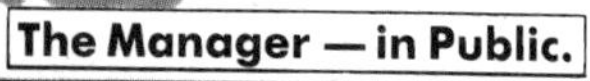

The Manager — in Public.

The Manager — in private!

The Autograph Hunter.

The Referee, as he sees himself.

The Referee as the Fans see him.

Not forgetting the Armchair Fan!

BABY CROCKETT
Bedtime, Baby!
Aw, Mum — Me's not sleepy!
Little boys go to bed when they're told.
I'll leave the light on. Night, Baby.
Rats!
Next day —
Me won't get put t'bed early tonight.
Look, Mum — Me's growed big!
So you have — we'll go for a meal to celebrate!

No high chair — Me wants a real chair!
Er . . . maybe the high chair after all. Me won't see my fish fingers an' chips!
Whassat? 'At's not fish fingers an' chips!
Fish fingers and chips is on the childrens menu. This is what big boys eat — liver and cabbage!
Me will get t'stay up an' watch telly, though.
Yes, there's a good movie on.
It's a h-h-horror!

Me's never been so glad to get to bed in all my life!
Big boys don't get the light left on.
MUM!
Me's only little! Me's not big at all.
Yes, you are . . .
. . . you're a big softie!
Aww!

HEARING the noises of unfamiliar animals being carried to him by the biting Arctic wind, the polar bear cub had wandered away from his den and his mother for the first time.

His mother was the mightiest and fiercest animal in the world, and when she was near he feared nothing. He walked softly through the late Spring snow until he came to the top of a hill which overlooked a small town. On the outskirts of the town, a travelling circus had camped for the night.

Cautiously he padded down the hill as the evening light began to fail. He entered the circus encampment, and walked past a pen of horses, from Arabia, wearing scarlet coats to protect them from the unfamiliar cold. He passed caged lions from the African plains and tigers from the jungles of Bengal. None were as fierce or strong as his mother. A circus dog sprang out from under a caravan, growling. It turned away, cowering, for although the cub was young the dog was no match for him.

Suddenly, before the cub, was the greatest mountain of flesh and bone he had ever seen. The great beast turned and stared at him and the cub ran away from the circus, and ran up the hill as snow began to fall, over frozen miles, until he came to the snowy den where his mother paced impatiently. She gave her cub a light cuff with one great paw, but she no longer seemed so awesome to him. For he had seen the elephant.

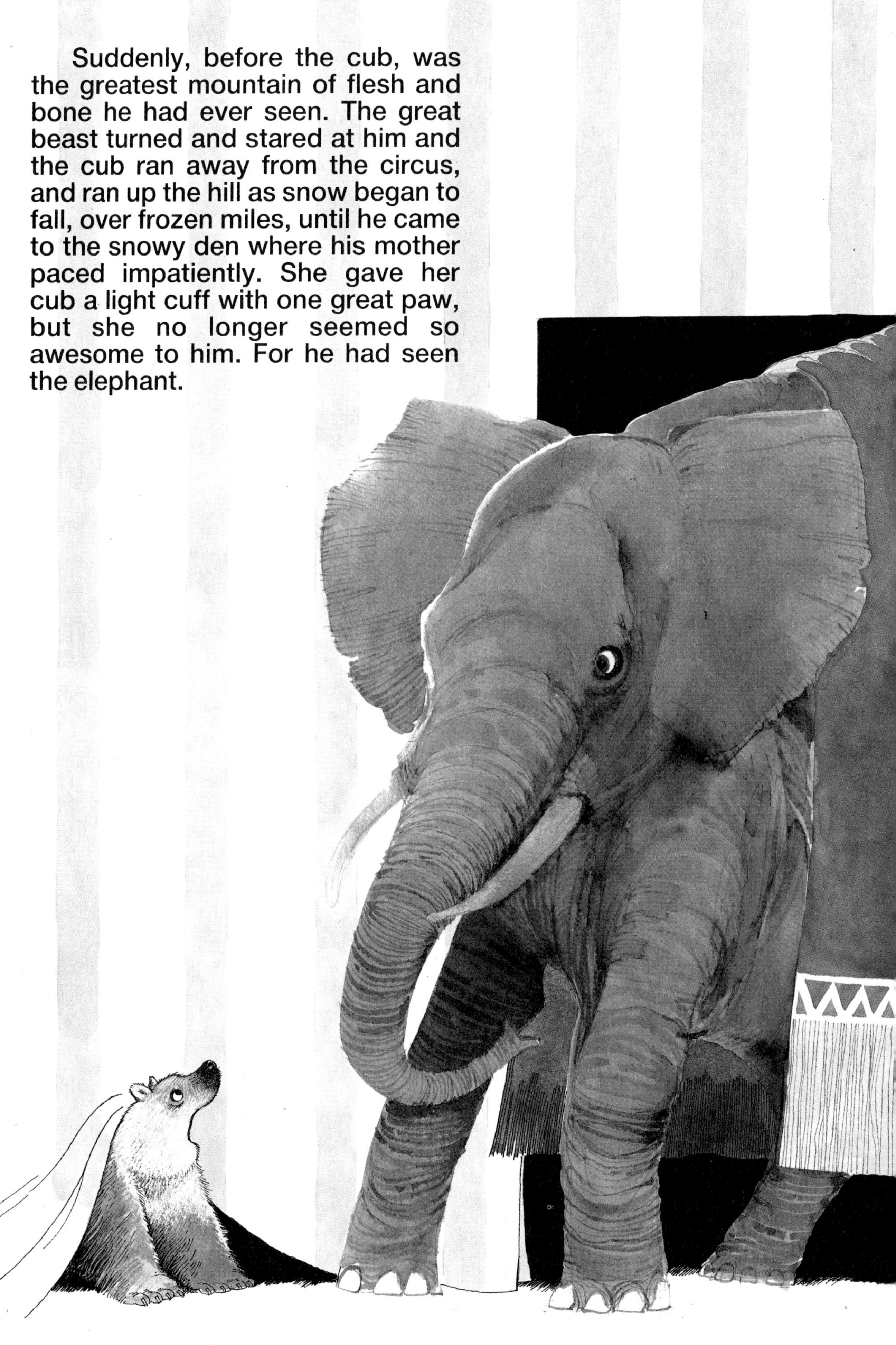

ADRIAN THE BARBARIAN
I'm goin' to our new leisure centre today.
Dunno how good an idea it is though.
ZAP!
LEISURE CENTRE
Well, at least the changing rooms look ok . . .
CHANGING ROOMS
. . . but I don't! They've changed me into an onion!
FLUME TUNNELS
I'll try the flumes first.
Whee!

Oh-oh! I don't fancy bein' a giant spider's dinner though!

But I have a cunning plan!

SOB!
Har! I'm obviously not very a-peeling any more!

Yahoo!
SPLOOSH!
SPLASH!

Yippee! I'm back to normal! It must be something . . .

. . . in the water! GULP!

SNAR
1 TON
LIFE GUARD
HELP!

LIFE GUARD
I'll save you — for my supper!
MARY CELESTE
Yelp!
SLURP!
SNAP!
was right! There IS something in the water! An' now I'm getting out of here!

The BADD LADS

Oh, no! We blundered into a field owned by a billy goat!

MISSED US!
THUD!

Hey, look! The bracelet!
PLOP!

Of course! We went up that tree to bird watch! Clever Badd lads!

Lovely pike.
More turnip?

Next day —
DEAR FISHERMAN HERE IS YOUR PIKE

And —
FANCY DRESS HIRE SHOP
FOR HIRE
Aw, how sweet! Those Badd lads aren't so bad after all!

POTSWORTH
and Co . . .
© 1994. H.B. Inc. S.K. plc. All rights reserved.
Meet Potsworth and the rest of the Midnight Patrol. Potsworth and his human friends are very special, for when they sleep they go off to the Dream Zone, the place where all our dreams come from!

Here's the Patrol — and Carter's reading a book about Irish legends . . .
IRISH LEGENDS
Listen to this. In Ireland there are little people called Leprechauns.
And, wow! Get this! Leprechauns bury pots of gold at the ends of rainbows! Weird dudes!
Hey, Rosie! You like a good argument — aren't you going to disagree with what's in Carter's book?
Not me! I've more important things to worry about!
You have?
What could be more important to Rosie than an argument?
I've got a MOLE on my wrist! It just grew there! How awful, how terrible! Total perfection of face and form — except for one rotten mole!
Hey, look! It's bedtime! Home we go, folks! I'll see you all in the Dream Zone later!

Off to sleep they go — to become the Midnight Patrol, and off to the Dream Zone they go.
In the Zone —
Hey, look at this tree — it's got beads instead of leaves!
Never mind beads! I'm so worried about my mole! Oh, worry, worry!
Yo! Look at that! A huge rainbow!
Maybe a Leprechaun has buried gold at the end of it!
Let's go find out!

Come on, before it fades!
Wait for me, folks!
I'm really worried about my mole!
Gasp! My arm — it's turning furry! And it's MOLE type fur!
Here we are!
We'll dig up the end of the rainbow now!
Hey, look at Rosie — she's turned into a human mole!
Gracious me! So she has!
It's not funny, fish face!
As you're now a mole, you can dig for the gold, Rosie!
Thanks a bundle!
Children can be so cruel, you know.

Hold on! If you dig up the pot of gold, the Leprechauns grant you a wish to get the gold back!
I'm digging! I'm digging!
You could wish to be human again! So get digging!
Who is that?!?
What's the problem, ma'am?
Your mole is digging up the foundations of the Rainbow Bridge! She'll bring the bridge down!
I'm Dorothy, guardian of the Rainbow Bridge.

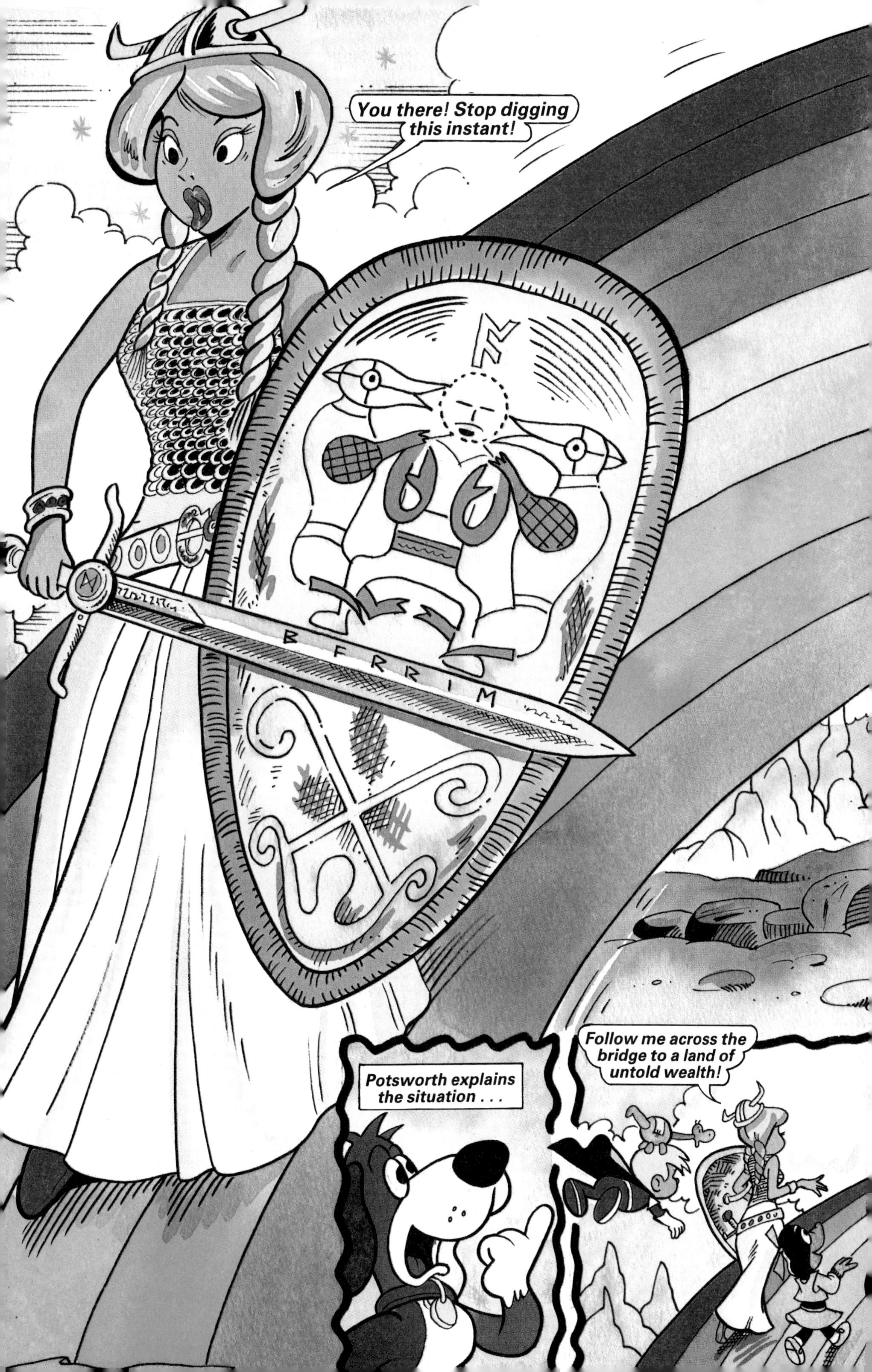

You there! Stop digging this instant!
B F R R I M
Potsworth explains the situation . . .
Follow me across the bridge to a land of untold wealth!

And I'll tell you the cure for your mole-ness.
What a weird place down below — it's got snow, rain sunshine, hurricanes —
Yes, the Rainbow Bridge crosses the chasm of Mixed Weather Forecasts.

Here we are, in the Land of Snow and Ice.
And here's the treasure.
Jewels — made of snow and ice!
You worried out loud about your mole, beside a Worry Bead tree. Those trees make your worries come true!
Now I understand! And I know the cure to your problem, Rosie!
Bye, Patrol! Thanks for not damaging the Rainbow Bridge!
We're rich, all those jewels!
Come on, Rosie, we've got to find that Worry Bead tree again!
Thanks, Dorothy!

At the tree —
Oh, worry, worry! I'm worried I might turn into a human again! Oh, worry, worry!
I'm worr — hey!
Hurrah! The tree has turned Rosie's worries on herself!
It's turned her human again!
You're back with us, Rosie!
Yes, and better looking than ever!
I fear, however, we've lost our jewels!
They've melted!

Yes, you see, Patrol, a rainbow is the sign of good weather after a storm. The good weather melted your treasure.
And, Patrol, there's no such thing as a Leprechaun!
And would that be so, Potsworth? I'm thinking, I am, that you don't know everything, my lad!

THE LIVING DINOSAUR

AROUND 65 million years ago the last of the dinosaurs were dying out as whole species vanished from the face of the earth, never to return. Why they became extinct is uncertain. Theories range from climate changes to the rise of egg eating mammals; whatever caused it, the age of the dinosaurs was coming to an end.
AT that time the greatest of all predators, Tyrannosaurus Rex, was chasing his prey and huge Pteranodon wheeled overhead. Meanwhile giants like Plesiosaur ploughed the great oceans, sharing prey with Coelocanth. But by 60 million years ago the dinosaurs were extinct . . . or so we thought.
THEN, in 1938, a living dinosaur was caught in coastal African waters! Coelocanth (pronounced see-lo-kanth), a primitive fish thought extinct for 60 million years, thrives there to this day! How many other dinosaurs are yet to be discovered in the wide oceans or deep in tropical rain forests?

ALL HAIL, 'TIS JULIUS BEEZER!

More power, Scotty!
BANG!
BONG!
BASH!
WALLOP!
The engine will no tak' the strain!

Er . . . we don't mind taking the occasional pet on on a cruise . . .
Yes, Cap'n?
SHIP'S LOG!

— but would you mind removing the elephant?
SINK!
S.S. TITANICUS

I'm at my holidayus destination. The exotic far northern country of Britannicus.
TO BRITAIN
WADE!

I came! I saw!

I hired a deckchair!
BLUSH!

What's that you have on?
That's woad.

And that's a woman woad!
Apparently his namus is Wodney.

Why am I the onlyus person on this beach?
SCRATCH!

'Cos the weather's so changeable.
Oh, no!

He's right! I think I'll go homus!

Hail, Caesar!
THUNDER!
CRACK!
SLEET!
HAIL!
Hail, sleet, snow! What a countryus!

Teecher Types
INK
I'm your new Form Master — and I wasn't born yesterday!
Careful opening that paint tube, Jones.
You'll just love this piece of romantic literature.
Quietly, Smith. Quietly!
SCIENCE ROOM
You're right. It IS making a strange noise.
1066
HISTORY
I suppose you think I'm an old fuddy-duddy.
It's really quite simple.
"Ee ba goom" is not a French phrase, Higgensworth!
bon jour
Je suis
tu es
il est
FRENCH
Right! Who will I put down for the 10 mile obstacle course?
WR

SHULA had taken the morning off school. How could she be expected to attend her class on such a bright blue Pacific morning, when it was just perfect for taking a long solitary walk along the white sands which fringed her island.

Suddenly her eyes fixed on what seemed to be a pile of rags lying on the beach. As she drew closer she could see that it was, in fact, a dolphin, washed up by the crashing surf.

Seagulls were jabbing at the dolphin's skin with their darting orange beaks. Waving her arms she shooed them away from their unmoving victim.

The dolphin's skin was beginning to burn and blister in the blazing morning sun.

She attempted to lift the dolphin, which was breathing softly, but it was far too heavy. She tried to drag it back to the sea, by its tail, but to no avail.

She couldn't go back to school for help, because her teacher would know she'd taken the morning off with no excuse, and she'd be in deep trouble. Stupid dolphin, anyway. If it didn't know enough to stay in the water, it didn't deserve to be saved. Right?

Wrong. Racing towards the school, to get help, as fast as her legs would carry her, Shula thought, "Well, what's a few hundred lines anyway . . ."

OVER THE
FENCE

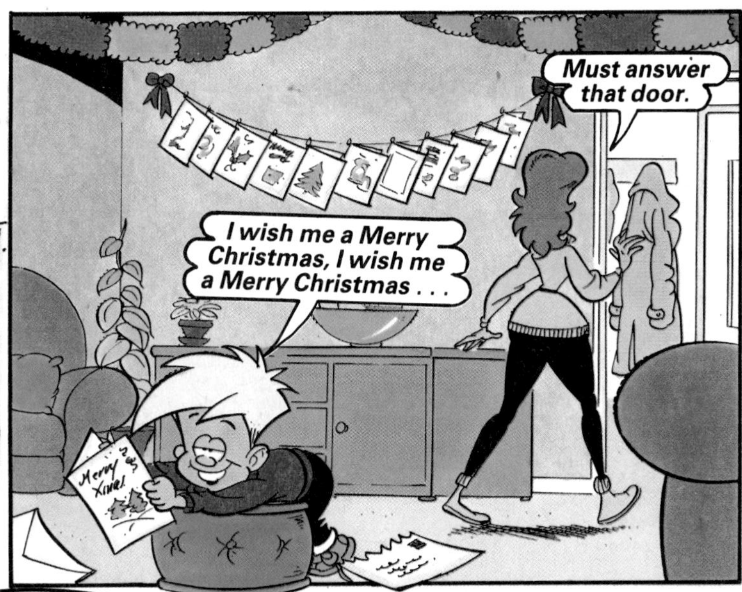
Must answer that door.
I wish me a Merry Christmas, I wish me a Merry Christmas . . .

PAIN
Whine!

YEOW!
Ooh! It's Lucy and her Dad with the tree.
Woops! Silly me. So sorry.

You two decorate the tree while we fix the turkey.
Yum!
Okay, Ma. Ooh! The pain!

C'mon, pipsqueak. We'd better get decoratin'.
If you say so, squirt.

You start with this.
WAAH!

ZOOM!
Eeks! I'm gonna splat you!
Oh, yeah?

TUG!
Gotcha!
OH, NO!
ZIP!

Mutter! Mumble! Mutter! Gnash!

You're in trouble now. The bell's gonna get ya.
What? This little bell here?

Nope! This huge one here.
DING! A LING!
Aargh!

Soon —
Ooh! That's very, very good, Eric.
Where's Lucy?
Well . . .

I'M UP HERE! HELP!
Don't worry, Sweetums. Daddy will save you.
You naughty boy, Eric.

Dear me.
What now?
Oi! You!
C'mere!

Ooh! That's nice.
Happy Christmas.
Ta! One for you, too.

Silly us. It was all just a misunderstanding.
Yes! Everything's fine now.
Cackle! Ta! Just what I always wanted.
Same here. Daft old Mum. There's no misunderstanding. Having somebody to fight with is the best prezzie ever.
TO ERIC
TO LUCY

RATS!
We need a holiday!
Yer! But where?
Somewhere hot, lotsa sunbathing!
Yer! Like this!
Wot else, though?
Swimmin'!
We need lotsa food, too!

BUZZ!
Like THAT!
BUZZ!
CHOMP!
Wot about a beach?

Fire buckets — instant beach, boys!
McNugget beach balls!

Nightlife, next!

Lend us yer ghetto blaster!

Rats! How vile!
PETS
What use is a disco without —

— GIRLS!
Well, birds!

Boogie on down!
Stop! Hold it!
THAT'S the place for our holidays!
Yer!
Wonderful, just right for us Rats!
The Scottish island called MUCK!
Och! Donald MacDonald, we're being invaded by Sassenach RATS!
'Tis a crime, Donald MacDonald MacCloud!
Z
Z

Tricky Dicky

I'll count that as two!

RECORD STORE

My friend and I would like to listen to this. We may purchase it.

Er . . . what friend?
This friend!

SNAKE!
Dirty great big snake!

Hah! It's a rubber snake. Still, that's three!

Morning.
Morning.

Hee-hee!

That's four!

KRISPIES' BIKE RACE
Hmm!

This'll slay 'em — literally!
DIVERSION

Suckers!
DIVERSION

And that's FIVE!
Argh!
Yaroo!
Mumsie!
PUBLIC SWIMMING POOL
Number six coming up!
Such grace. Such poise.
Such a belly

Shriek!
SMACK!
Howl!
Six! Four to go!
PUBLIC SWI ING POOL

CAR WASH

No! No!
Four left!

Boo-hoo! Somebody put paint in the car wash!
Good trick, eh?

CAR WASH
Look at 'em — all come to complain about little me!

That's number seven!

BURGER DRIVE-IN
Quietly does it!

Can I take your order, sir?

Two burgers, no onions. Hot dog. French fries all round.
Coming up!

Have a nice day.
That was quick!

Shriek! The box is full of ants and beetles!
And a SKUNK!
WAY OUT

Abandon car!
There goes number eight! Only two left.

This one's gonna be a biggy!
TROLLEYS

Excuse me! Congratulations! You are our one millionth customer.
As our millionth customer, you get to fill this trolley with as many goods as you can from our shelves, ABSOLUTELY FREE OF CHARGE!
But hurry, Madam! You have only two minutes in which to fill your trolley, so GO! GO! GO!
Gangway! I want this! I want that!
Human greed — rely on it!
Hoi! Come back here!
It's all mine! All mine, I tell you!

PAY for this lot? Certainly not! All of this is FREE! The man told me so!
I don't care if a little green martian told you so! PAY UP!
Music to my ears! One more trick to go!

Now, what's this last trick gonna be . . ?

Oh, no you don't!

Nine tricks in one day! One to go, it says here. What's going on? Why ten tricks in one day?

'Cos I've checked my records. Up till today I'd done 990 tricks this year. I just wanted to make it 1000 before Christmas!

Well, now I'M here, there'll be no more tricks! You'll NEVER get to 1000!

That's what he thinks! The last trick was I let Dad babble on till he ran out of story! Now he can't punish me! 1000 tricks are up! Have a nice Christmas, folks!
Tricky litt

The
BANANA
BUNCH

You could do with losin' some weight.
Nonsense! I'm in great shape an' I'll prove it!
DISGUSTED!
BAARP! BELCH!
SLOO!
BLACK PUDDEN BIRYANI
KIPPER VINDALOO
BANGER BHOONA
CURRY COLA
FRIED EGG BHAJI

I'm not convinced. Tiny, if you'd be so kind . . .
BIG BREATH!

No probs, Brainy.
PURPLE STRAIN!
POKE! PROD! TICKLE!

As I suspected — poor, ol' Tiny's been belly-slammed!
WHEEZO!
GAASP! PHOOO!
SPLAMM!

Tiny's not in great shape now.
But Fatty will be — with exercise.
WAFER-THIN WAFFLE!
PEEL!

Swimmin' will make you lose weight — to Banana Pond!
So —
SU-UCK! CHIRRUP!
WORM FLAVOUR FIZZ
Mercy! I had a bath last month!
BLOATED BLITHER!
BANANA POND
HAUL! DRAG!
WOBBLE!
FAR TOO FAT!
Stop whinin', Fatty!
TRUNDLE! SQUEAK!
PLUNGE!
Rats! There's not enough room for Fatty and the water!
FAT-FACED GUFFAW!
FAR TOO FAT!
Soon —
SWEAT! PUFF! PANT!
This'll make you lose weight, Fatty. And we're bein' kind — it's all downhill from here on.
PROPERTY OF YOGGO YOGHURT COMPANY.
SU-UCK! MOOO!
HUGE BLUBBERY BELLY JIGGLING LIKE A GIGANTIC JELLY!
BANANAMOBILE
CUD COLA
TOWN UMPTEEN MILES
RATTLE!
VUMM!

Oh, bother! I knew this would happen — I couldn't see my feet for my belly!
FEED UDDER END!
PUFF! SWEAT!
MILLET
Ulp!
HORRIBLE FEELING OF IMPENDING DOOM!
TRIP!
BaNaNaMoBiLe

BOUNCE!
RUMBLE!
ROLL!
SPLINTER! CRUNCH! SQUIDGE! MANGLE!

Shortly —
We've all lost some weight now . . .

. . . Fatty! Last seen headin' for London! If anybody spots him, KEEP OUT OF HIS WAY!
BLITHER! TWITTER!
DISTANT RUMBLE!

GREY MOON and his two elder brothers left their tepee one crisp October morning. Arrow, his oldest brother, pointed to an old grey wolf which watched them from a hill about half a mile distant.

"Today, little brother, we will teach you the skills of tracking," he told Grey Moon.

The three youths ran to where the wolf had been standing. Grey Moon was first to find its footprints in the dew dampened earth.

"Now we can start," he said.

They followed the wolf's footprints until they came to the banks of a fast flowing river. The tracks stopped at the water's edge. Cloud, the middle brother, shook his head sadly.

"I've lost the trail. I'll return home."

Young Grey Moon was delighted. "And to think you were going to tell me about tracking."

Grey Moon walked, knee deep, downstream, until the wolf's prints re-appeared on the other side of the river bank.

"He walked down the river to put us off his trail," he said, knowingly.

GREY MOON and his oldest brother followed the trail with renewed enthusiasm, until they reached a thick wood. Arrow shook his head. "I've lost his trail. I too must return home."

Grey Moon was delighted. "Even you can't teach me about tracking." The youngster pointed to a broken branch. "Look, he came this way — and then through the wood."

Alone now, he followed the trail through the dense wood until, in a clearing, he came face to face with the old wolf, which would have been wary of all three brothers, but not of only one. The wolf snarled at Grey Moon. The youth ran flat out through the wood, over grassland, across the river and down the hill until, breathless, he arrived back at his village where his laughing brothers were waiting. "You see, we DID teach you something. Never track a wolf unless you're sure you want to catch up with it, first."

Blinky

Who are you looking at, ugly mug?

I'm busy. Go to the shops and get me —
Yes, dad?

Hi, Mum.

Hello, Mrs Smith.

This must be your lovely daughter, Amanda. Good morning, my dear.

Didn't know you owned a poodle, Mrs Smith.
PAT!

Snort! I'll kill him!

TOWN CENTRE
COUNTRYSIDE

COUNTRYSIDE
Soon be in the town centre.

Ah, the butcher's shop.
HOME GROWN PRODUCE

Half a pound of bacon, unsmoked, please.
Don't have any bacon.
HOME

No bacon? No bacon? Good grief, man, next you'll be telling me you've no mince either!
Correct.
HOME GROWN PRODUCE

Well, I'm not shopping HERE again!
That's a relief.

I say! What a jolly fine rocking horse you have there, lad.
PORKY

I haven't seen one of these in ages. May I have a rock?

Eh?
PORKY

Oh, dear! I've made a ghastly error — this isn't a rocking horse — it's a Shetland pony!

Here comes Blinky.
Did he get that bacon I asked for?

And then some!
Whoa, horse! Whoa!

MACBOOM was the last of the great Scottish giants. He was stronger than an army. He could lift an ox in each hand. He would uproot a tree and comb his hair with it. He could crush boulders in his bare hands.

But he had grown bored. There had been nothing new to challenge his great might for twenty years.

He nailed up a notice in the nearby village, promising a bag of gold to anyone who could defeat him in a test of might.

THE villagers shook their heads. None among them could hope to defeat the giant and win his gold. Except for one small skinny boy called Jamie.

Jamie said to the giant, "I accept your challenge. I can lift something you can't." The giant laughed. Jamie dropped a pea on the ground and told the giant to pick it up. Hard as he tried, his huge clumsy fingers could not grasp the tiny pea.

Jamie then picked it up with ease, winning the bag of gold.

Jamie pointed to his head and told the giant — "You've got to be strong in here, too!"

GEEZER
A million sovs? That's for me, 'cos they are all fakes, y'know!
NEWS
£1,000,000 IF YOU CAN EXPLAIN CORN CIRCLES!
I'm gonna wait till I hear someone faking up a circle.
Aha! Now I'll —
RUSTLE!
LEAP!
— leap out and nab 'em!

Would now be a good time to say "oops"?
SNORT!
I'll take that as a yes!
And YEOW as well!
BAM!
FLASH!
Doofyah!
CRASH!
Doh! I'm not well — I'm seeing things!

We're not so sure. Maybe they'll believe him when they see our corn Geezer!

All that fame! AND MONEY! GONE!

RN.

THE NUMSKULLS

Which will I visit — the opera or the panto?
THEATRE 1 NOW SHOWING The BARBER of CLEETHORPES
THEATRE 2 NOW SHOWING Mother Goosie

Opera definitely. A bit of culture.

Forget culture, chum! It's panto for me!

Panto here we come!

I want opera too! It's soothing on the ears.

Heads, opera. Tails, panto.

STING!

I love Christmas, me!

What a target!

And I got the Christmas tree fairy!
Ooh, sore!

You can sting all sorts at Christmas!

What a target!
SANTA

That one hit gnome! Home-gnome, geddit? Oh, please yourselves!

No-one is safe from Sting!
Except, perhaps, him!
Easy peasy! Prepare to scream in mortal agony!
FAP!
Glub!
Snow use stinging me!
Bah! A snowman!

TA-TA!
BYE-EE!
Au Revoir!
Boogie-on!
See ya!
TATTY-BYE!